NS ALIVE

Sea Dragons

by David Schach

BELLWETHER MEDIA • MINNEAPOLIS, MN

BLASTOFF!
2
READERS

Note to Librarians, Teachers, and Parents:

Blastoff! Readers are carefully developed by literacy experts and combine standards-based content with developmentally appropriate text.

Level 1 provides the most support through repetition of high-frequency words, light text, predictable sentence patterns, and strong visual support.

Level 2 offers early readers a bit more challenge through varied simple sentences, increased text load, and less repetition of high-frequency words.

Level 3 advances early-fluent readers toward fluency through increased text and concept load, less reliance on visuals, longer sentences, and more literary language.

Whichever book is right for your reader, Blastoff! Readers are the perfect books to build confidence and encourage a love of reading that will last a lifetime!

This edition first published in 2007 by Bellwether Media.

No part of this publication may be reproduced in whole or in part without written permission of the publisher. For information regarding permission, write to Bellwether Media Inc., Attention: Permissions Department, Post Office Box 1C, Minnetonka, MN 55345-9998.

Library of Congress Cataloging-in-Publication Data
Schach, David.
  Sea dragons / by David Schach.
    p. cm. – (Oceans alive)
Summary: "Simple text and supportive full-color photographs introduce beginning readers to sea dragons. Intended for kindergarten through third grade students"

  Includes bibliographical references and index.
  ISBN-13: 978-1-60014-055-6 (hardcover : alk. paper)
  ISBN-10: 1-60014-055-6 (hardcover : alk. paper)
  1. Sea dragons—Juvenile literature. I. Title.

  QL638.S9S32 2007
  597'.679–dc22   2006036986

Contents

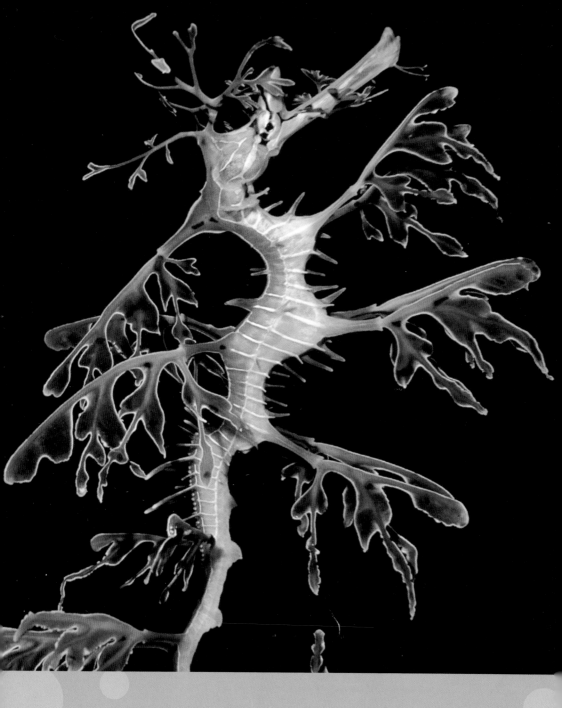

Sea dragons are a kind
of fish.

They live in shallow water
along the ocean shore.

Sea dragons live near the
coast of **Australia**.

6

Most sea dragons are about as long as a ruler. Some can grow to be as long as your arm.

A sea dragon has hard plates on its body. It does not have **scales** like most fish have.

A sea dragon has big,
round eyes.

mouth

A sea dragon has a long mouth. It has no teeth.

The mouth works like a straw.

There are two kinds of
sea dragons.

This is a **weedy sea dragon**. It has flaps of skin that look like weeds.

This is a **leafy sea dragon**.
Many flaps of skin cover
its body.

Its flaps of skin sway gently
like leaves under the water.

fins

A sea dragon has small **fins**. Its fins are so thin you can see through them.

A sea dragon uses its fins to move slowly through the water.

A sea dragon hides well.

It can change color to
match its **surroundings**.

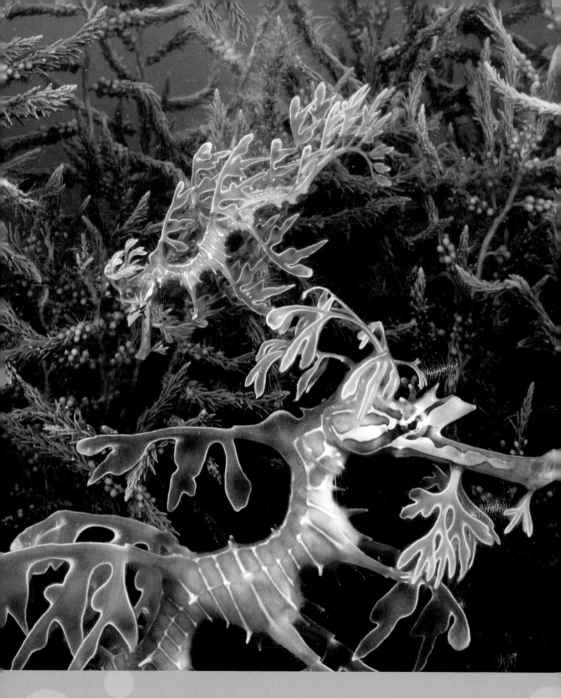

A sea dragon swims among the
ocean plants. Its flaps of skin
help it **blend** with the plants.

A sea dragon is an amazing ocean animal.

Glossary

Australia—the smallest continent in the world

blend—when something looks so much like the things around it that it is hard to see

coast—the land along the edge of an ocean

fins—thin parts that stick out from a fish's body; a fish uses fins to move through the water.

leafy sea dragon—a kind of sea dragon; a leafy sea dragon has many flaps of skin on its body that look like leaves.

scales— small, hard plates that cover the skin of a fish

surroundings—the area around something

weedy sea dragon—a kind of sea dragon; a weedy sea dragon has fewer flaps of skin on its body than a leafy sea dragon.

To Learn More

AT THE LIBRARY
Rhodes, Mary Jo. *Seahorses and Sea Dragons*.
Danbury, Conn.: Scholastic, 2006.

Herriges, Ann. *Sea Horses*. Minneapolis, Minn.:
Bellwether Media, 2007.

ON THE WEB
Learning more about sea dragons
is as easy as 1, 2, 3.

1. Go to www.factsurfer.com

2. Enter "sea dragons" into search box.

3. Click the "Surf" button and you will see a list of
   related web sites.

With factsurfer.com, finding more information is
just a click away.

Index

The photographs in this book are reproduced through the courtesy of: Visual & Written SL/Alamy, front cover; Mark Conlin/Getty Images, p. 4; Darryl Torckler/Getty Images, p. 5; Ximagination, p. 6; Takaji Ochi/V&W/imagequestmarine.com, p. 7; Arco Images/Alamy, pp. 8-9; Ferenc Cegledi, p. 10; Stephen Frink Collection/Alamy, p. 11; Johnny Lye, pp. 12-13; Visual & Written SL/Alamy, p. 14; Brandon Cole Marine Photography/Alamy, p. 15; Bruce Coleman Inc./Alamy, p. 16; Justin Kim, p. 17; Roger Steene/imagequestmarine.com, pp. 18-19; David Fleetham/Alamy, p. 20; Scott Tuason/imagequestmarine.com, p. 21.